UNMERITED FAVOR

101 QUOTES OF WISDOM, INSPIRATION, AND GOD'S GRACE

Grace LaJoy Henderson

Unmerited Favor   Grace LaJoy Henderson

UNMERITED FAVOR:
101 QUOTES OF WISDOM, INSPIRATION, AND GOD'S GRACE
Copyright ©2013. Grace LaJoy Henderson
Published by Inspirations by Grace LaJoy
www.gracelajoy.com

ISBN: 978-0-9829404-6-4

All rights reserved. No portion of this book may be copied, reproduced or transmitted in any form without prior written permission from the publisher.

Printed in the United States of America

Favorite Quotes from Others

"Don't EVER say anything negative about yourself!"

~ **Joyce Meyer**

"*Everything* happens when you find your purpose and *nothing* happens until you do."

~**T.D. Jakes**

"It's not over until you win!"

~**Les Brown**

"A woman's heart should be so lost in God that a man must seek Him in order to find her."

~**Maya Angelou**

"You were made by God and for God and until you understand that, life will never make sense."

~ **Rick Warren**

Foreword

Sometimes a positive word is all we need to get over a difficult moment. **UNMERITED FAVOR** offers inspiration and encouragement to those looking for an uplifting word during a down or lonely time. The quotes in this book will also make great conversation starters or ice-breakers at your next gathering.

Vera A. McKissic
Cornerstone Church
Arlington, Texas

TABLE OF CONTENTS

Introduction	1
Quotes with Titles	3
Quotes of Wisdom	9
Quotes of Inspiration	17
Quotes of God's Grace	25
Prayer of Salvation	34
Books and Resources	37

Introduction

The quotes in this book were inspired through Dr. Grace LaJoy, who wrote and spoke them over a period of a several years. Now she has compiled them all in this one book entitled, UNMERITED FAVOR, which is the definition of "Grace", her own name. "Unmerited" is that which we do not deserve.

Many of the quotes in this book represent God's grace, love, mercy, and forgiveness. The positive message of each quote offers edification, encouragement, and empowerment. The author's purpose is to share wisdom and inspiration while expressing God's UNMERITED FAVOR towards us.

Unmerited Favor   Grace LaJoy Henderson

Quotes with Titles

Unmerited Favor			Grace LaJoy Henderson

GOD'S UNMERITED FAVOR
I thank God that He doesn't bless me according to *my* goodness, but *His* goodness; not according to *my* faithfulness, but according to *His* faithfulness; not according to *my* love for others; but according to *His* love for me; not according to *my* attitude, but according to *His* grace and mercy towards me.

HEARTACHE/LOVE
Heartache, Headache, Pain, Fear, Hurt, etc. These are some of the things we have to go through in order to get to *Love, Happiness, Fame, Goodness, Paradise, etc.* ....and be strong enough to handle it when we get there.

HYPOCRITES
Some people refuse to go to church because they say there are too many "hypocrites" in the church. I say, if all the "hypocrites" left the church, there would be *no one* left in the church; for, we *all* have sinned and come short of the glory of God. We do not attend church because *we* are so good, but, because *God* is so good.

EVERYTHING
Everything that feels good is not always good for us; and Everything that's good for us does not always feel good.

SOMETIMES
Sometimes I wish my mother would not have left me when I was two. Sometimes I wish I could have at least found her after she left...the longing just to know her has been excruciating! But, then I am reminded that if my life had been different, I would not be the person I am today...and I like who I am!

DIVINE CONNECTIONS
It seems everywhere I go, I end up connected with someone who I am able to help get to the next level and/or who is able to help me get to the next level.

UNDESERVED LOVE
As much as I would love to hate the person who hurt me deeply, I can't. God won't let me. I have to love them. I can't help but to think kind and prayerful thoughts about them. Not because I am so good, or because they are so good, but, because GOD is so good.

TRY GOD

Satan will tell you that when you choose God you will have to give up some things that you may not feel ready to give up. But, what he does not tell you is all that you will GAIN by choosing God. Try God today!

MAN OF HONOR

There's nothing more attractive than a man of honor: an Honest man who says what he means and means what he says; a Dependable man who does what he says he is going to do; a Trustworthy man whose word is his bond, and whatsoever he says can be taken to the bank and traded for cash!

OUR CALLING

We have to know where our gifts and talents lie. We can be a songwriter, but, not a singer. We can be a poet, but, not a spoken word artist. We can be funny, but, not be a comedian. We can inspire audiences, but, not be a speaker. We must operate in the area of our calling.

OUR ANOINTING

Sometimes people will tell us, since you do THIS so well, then you should consider doing THAT. It is okay to CONSIDER it. But, when it is all said and done, we need to be aware of our strengths, know what our gifts and talents are, and work within our anointing.

HEALING
When we get to the place where we stop blaming other people for our downfalls and heartbreaks (regardless of how imperfect other people may truly be; and regardless of the role they may have played in our problem); and begin to recognize, admit and confront our own issues, then that is where we will find healing, restoration, and deliverance for our own soul.

GROWING OLD
We ought to be thankful whenever God allows us to see another birthday! Seeing so many people fighting the physical signs of aging, my children's wonderful grandmother often said, "The only way you don't grow old is if you die young!"

MINISTRY
I believe that to speak only that which has already been spoken or only that with which others will agree, is to leave no room for one's own ministry.

Quotes of Wisdom

Unmerited Favor   Grace LaJoy Henderson

Unmerited Favor   Grace LaJoy Henderson

Everything I learned yesterday will be used to help others tomorrow.

~~~

If we can't be a help to others, then what are we good for?

~~~

Don't ignore the bike, car, train, plane, helicopter, or even the canoe while waiting for your ship to come in.

~~~

Cry about the problem *later*, but, let's spend *right now* finding a solution.

~~~

God wants our undivided attention.

~~~

The more I learn the more I realize how much I don't know.

Looking back on life, and realizing how much could be done differently if given another chance.

~~~

Our testimony to others does not have to be perfect, just honest and sincere.

~~~

After a serious relationship, it is important to take *all* of the time needed to heal *before* entering into a new relationship.

~~~

It takes so much more than a good meal for a man to be happy and content.

~~~

The more you are able to do for yourself, the less you will have to pay someone else to do for you.

~~~

Unmerited Favor   Grace LaJoy Henderson

Some people buy what they want, then beg for what they need.

~~~

Keep a good name and good credit.

~~~

Paying a bill *on time* is just as important as paying the bill.

~~~

Not being married, or not being in a serious relationship, doesn't necessarily make a person "single" or "available".

~~~

There is nothing more attractive than an honest person.

~~~

Be a person of your word and don't expect any less from others.

Unmerited Favor   Grace LaJoy Henderson

If we *always* have a problem with others, the problem just may be within ourselves.

~~~

The *only* way to begin is to get started.

~~~

We should live our lives in a way in which we have nothing to hide.

~~~

An insincere person who *constantly* apologizes might be a sorry person.

~~~

If a person does not respect you *before* you sin to impress them, they will not respect you *afterward*s.

~~~

Unmerited Favor   Grace LaJoy Henderson

We are not required to open the door just because someone knocks...nor run to the phone just because it rings.

~~~

Always leave in a way that coming back would be welcomed.

~~~

If we honor and respect marriage and are faithful to God, then we will honor, respect, and be faithful to our mate regardless of circumstances and temptations.

~~~

I believe college students should choose a degree plan and course work that is easy and enjoyable for *them*.

~~~

Tell a student that the subject they desire to study is not good enough and they could end up studying *nothing*.

Unmerited Favor   Grace LaJoy Henderson

If my life does not speak for me, I might as well keep my mouth shut.

~~~

If you don't like me for who I am then you don't like me.

~~~

Discipline means to teach, not scream, holler and hit.

~~~

Do you feel confused about it? Then wait until you have peace before proceeding...

~~~

Failing is a learning experience.

~~~

Unshared knowledge is useless.

~~~

Quotes of Inspiration

Unmerited Favor Grace LaJoy Henderson

Unmerited Favor   Grace LaJoy Henderson

God can do *anything*, at *anytime*, through *anybody*.

~~~

If you are reading this, you are beautiful!

~~~

Hold others to a high standard and they will "rise up" to the challenge.

~~~

Most people are honest, sincere, upstanding, and of good character.

~~~

As long as we have breath it's not too late to pursue our dreams and reach our goals.

~~~

So, I did something kind for a stranger one day...and he said, "Thank You!" "This is the *only* nice thing that has happened to me all day!"

Unmerited Favor   Grace LaJoy Henderson

If you are reading this, you are a treasure, a jewel, a gem!

~~~

It costs nothing to be nice and kind.

~~~

Every struggle of yester-year has prepared us for the inspiration we will share in future years.

~~~

My past teachings will be used to empower others in the future.

~~~

Praying that God will continue to use the work HE gave me to do to be a blessing to others.

~~~

If you are a writer, then, write it as soon as the inspiration comes. Don't say, "I'll write it later".

Unmerited Favor   Grace LaJoy Henderson

If you are talking about it you probably are not doing it.

~~~

It is always nice when reality finally sets in and long awaited answers to questions are clear.

~~~

Nothing happens until you get started.

~~~

It is truly a blessing to finally see the light after being in the dark about something for a period of time.

~~~

Gotta keep movin' forward! Gotta keep pressin' forward!

~~~

Not sure exactly what God has in store for my life, but, I am excited about it!

With God, we have the power to do anything!

~~~

Do not wait until you can do more, take the little that you have and do *something* with it.

~~~

If you have a gift, use it! If you have inspiration, share it! Do not wait around to be *discovered* by a mere person.

~~~

Time will pass whether you fulfill your goals or not. So, go ahead and begin the process of accomplishing your goals!

~~~

Families are worth everything we go through to keep them together.

~~~

You don't have to be strong, just unstoppable.

Praying for God's perfect will in *every* aspect of your life.

~~~

Time spent complaining could be used for learning and teaching.

~~~

Do you want to know yourself better? Consult with God, your maker.

~~~

WE are history-makers. When future historians research THIS era, it is OUR contribution to the world that they will find.

Quotes of God's Grace

Unmerited Favor					Grace LaJoy Henderson

Unmerited Favor   Grace LaJoy Henderson

God has the ability, and the power, to protect us even when our immaturity places us in harm's way.

~~~

If we hurt someone, and then apologize, they may accept the apology and forgive us, but, it will naturally take time for their wound to heal.

~~~

Without God, His mercy, and His favor, I am nothing!

~~~

God loves us in spite of *our* mess and, through *Him*, we can love others in spite of *their* mess.

~~~

God can help us to look beyond the faults of others and see their need for prayer.

~~~

Unmerited Favor   Grace LaJoy Henderson

When God is in it, it just feels right and there is peace.

~~~

If ALL of our secrets were uncovered, would others still think fondly of us?

~~~

God knows what He wants to do with the gift He placed in you. Just be open and willing.

~~~

Nothing, or *no one*, in this world has more power than God?

~~~

If God allowed you to wake up this morning, then this is a blessed day.

~~~

All people should be respected and honored even when it is not deserved.

Unmerited Favor   Grace LaJoy Henderson

I know it doesn't seem fair, but, God loves that person who hurt you just as much as He loves you...

~~~

There is power in giving! True giving requires nothing in return.

~~~

Regardless of how dirty we are, God can clean us up.

~~~

You are just as special and important now as you were before you sinned or made that mistake.

~~~

I thank and praise God that broken hearts are mendable.

~~~

Thank God for friends who know *when* to pray, *what* to pray, and *how* to pray!

~~~

We don't serve God because WE are so good, but, because HE is so good...

~~~

We should forgive. Not because it is deserved, but, because God has forgiven us.

~~~

The trial that you are going through is only temporary. You *will* rise above it.

~~~

God's power is greater than *anything* you can ever go through.

~~~

True ministry is sharing God's love and the plan of salvation, and it does not require money.

Unmerited Favor   Grace LaJoy Henderson

Ministry that is shared through word of mouth, through actions, and through loving kindness, does not cost anything.

~~~

Honor others even though they are imperfect... we all are.

~~~

We should refrain from blaming others for our problems, they have their own.

~~~

We must be careful about how we judge others. Sometimes, the *only* way to understand the hardships of others is to experience them for ourselves.

~~~

If we all got what we deserved, we'd ALL be dead today.

~~~

Unmerited Favor   Grace LaJoy Henderson

It is good to apologize and ask for forgiveness.

~~~

With God we have *everything*, without Him we have *nothing*.

~~~

Christianity is not about religion, but, about knowing, accepting, displaying, and sharing God's love.

~~~

If God blessed us according to *our own* goodness we would *have* nothing and *be*
nothing.

~~~

Do right. Not for a blessing, but, for a closer relationship with God.

~~~

Unmerited Favor   Grace LaJoy Henderson

I believe God blesses us so that we can be a blessing to others.

~~~

Praise God for His unmerited favor, unexplainable miracles, unlimited peace, unspeakable joy, unstoppable blessings, untoppable grace, unending mercy, and undying love!

~~~

"Alter Call" is the most important part of the church service.

~~~

That moment when the preacher has preached and now it is time to accept the invitation to receive God's forgiveness...

The Prayer of Salvation

I cannot end this book about UNMERITED FAVOR without offering you the opportunity to accept God's grace and invite Jesus Christ into your heart, if you have not already done so. God loves us so much that He allowed His son Jesus Christ to die for our sins so that we can have everlasting life. (John 3:16). We sin when we do not do what God tells us to do; and sin separates us from God. (Isaiah 59:2).

The Bible says that if you confess with your mouth the Lord Jesus and believe in your heart that God has raised Him from the dead, you will be saved! (Romans 10:9). You can ask Jesus Christ to come and live in your heart right now! If you desire forgiveness for your sins and would like to invite Jesus Christ to come into your life, then pray these words with me:

"Jesus, I confess that I am a sinner in need of salvation. I acknowledge You as Lord and I believe that You are God's son. Thank You for dying so that my sins can be forgiven. I believe that You are still alive today. Please come into my life and take full control of it. I accept Your forgiveness for my sin. Thank You for giving me eternal life and for the gift of the Holy Spirit. Amen"

If you prayed the prayer of salvation with me, accepting God's forgiveness through His Son Jesus Christ, you are now a part of the family of God! Your sins have been forgiven and you have eternal life with Christ. The Bible says anyone who belongs to Christ becomes a new person. The old life goes away and a new life begins. So, as time goes on, and you continue to follow Jesus Christ, your attitudes and actions will begin to change. (2 Corinthians 5:17).

If you prayed the prayer of salvation with me, then there are *three* things that you need: A Bible, a prayer partner, and a church home. *A Bible* is God's Word and it is the primary way that He speaks to us. (John 1:1). *A prayer partner* is important because prayer is the primary way that we speak to God. When two or more people pray together God is with them. (Matthew 18:20). *A church home* is important because God instructs us to be around other believers, which is a great way to continue to grow in our faith in God. (Hebrews 10:25).

If you prayed the prayer of salvation with me, you now have a testimony to share with others and you are now equipped to begin walking, with confidence, in God's UNMERITED FAVOR!

Unmerited Favor Grace LaJoy Henderson

Other Books and Resources published by Inspirations by Grace LaJoy

A Gifted Child in Foster Care: *A Story of Resilience*
(Book, Teacher's Guide, Student Workbook)

Writer's Breakthrough:
Steps To Copyright and Publish Your Own Book
(Book)

More Than Mere Words: *Poetry That Ministers*
(Christian Poetry Book)

Social Inspirations: *Christian Quotes for Life*
by Aric J. Henderson

Poetic Empowerment (Spoken Word CD)

Poetic Book Series
Diversity in our Schools, Diversity in our Workplace
The Bad Butt Kids, He's Worth It

Sexual Purity and the Young Woman:
A Guide to Sexual Purity (Book)

Understanding Each Other:
A Guide for Parents and their Children (Book)

My Automobile Dealership (Book)

Diversity and My Credit Union (Book)

An Urgent Call to the Power of Ministry:
Realizing your ministry through your life experiences (Book)

Tapping Into the Gifts, Talents, and Learning Styles of Special Education Students by Arlivia S. White and Grace LaJoy Henderson (Book)

A New Kind of Hustle: *Finding Success in the Midst of Obstacles* by Sugar Lee Lewis, PhD with Grace LaJoy Henderson (Book-Available in Soft and Hard cover)

To learn more please visit us online at

www.gracelajoy.com

www.ingramcontent.com/pod-product-compliance
Lightning Source LLC
Chambersburg PA
CBHW071846290426
44109CB00017B/1941